mabo

maboclothier.com

A PEARL
OF LIGHT

CLAM™ PENDANT
Introducing the award-winning Clam™ pendant from Fritz Hansen, designed by Ahm and Lund. Mouth blown opal glass and brushed brass come together – and move apart – to create elegant and ambient lighting for dining and living spaces.

FRITZ HANSEN

EDITOR IN CHIEF
Harriet Fitch Little

EDITOR
John Burns

ART DIRECTOR
Staffan Sundström

DESIGN DIRECTOR
Alex Hunting

ILLUSTRATORS
Espen Friberg
Albert Tercero

**ADVERTISING,
SALES & DISTRIBUTION
DIRECTOR**
Edward Mannering

ADVERTISING MANAGER
Jessica Gray

**STUDIO &
PROJECT MANAGER**
Susanne Buch Petersen

DIGITAL MANAGER
Cecilie Jegsen

PROOFREADER
Taahir Husain

PUBLICATION DESIGN
Alex Hunting Studio

DESIGN ASSISTANT
Abbie Lilley

WORDS
Allyssia Alleyne
Danielle Campoamor
Jill Ceder
Jennifer Chen
Ed Cumming
Robert Ito
Liz Kleinrock
Andy Morris
Justin Myers
Rudri Bhatt Patel
Robyn Price Pierre
Emma Scott-Child
Mindy Thomas
Annick Weber
Tom Whyman

PHOTOGRAPHY & STYLING
Gustav Almestål
Nick Riley Bentham
Rodrigo Carmuega
Cayce Clifford
Ruth Higginbotham
Sarah Hingley
Pernilla Löfberg
Armin Tehrani

EDITORIAL BOARD
Shanicia Boswell
Liz Kleinrock
David Michael Perez
Robyn Price Pierre
Emma Scott-Child

PUBLISHER
Chul-Joon Park

COVER ILLUSTRATION
Espen Friberg

ISSUE 02
Kindling is published biannually by Ouur ApS, Amagertorv 14B, 2, 1160 Copenhagen, Denmark. Printed by Park Communications Ltd in London, United Kingdom. Color reproduction by Park Communications Ltd in London, United Kingdom. All rights reserved.

CONTACT US
If you have questions or comments, please write to us at *info@kinfolk.com*. For advertising and partnership inquiries, get in touch at *kindling@kinfolk.com*

Mushroom

Mushroom Lamp

tf

ISSUE TWO

With Issue One of *Kindling*, we set out to make a magazine that celebrates the humor, adventure and intellectual stimulation that comes with raising a child. In this second issue, those same values are given shape in an interview with Alison Gopnik: the acclaimed developmental psychologist and philosopher who has dedicated her career to proving the assertion that parenting doesn't mean doing "a whole bunch of things in order to make the child come out a particular way." As she tells Robert Ito on page 58, caring for a child means nurturing a relationship "that will let that person go out and discover the world for themselves."

This spirit of curiosity fuels our second issue, which is themed around the body. In our more lighthearted features we're celebrating the fashion potential of hi-vis outfits (p.34), getting creative with body casts and crutches (p.80), practicing drawing with our feet (p.110) and—most importantly—learning the difference between a fart and a burp (p.76). There are also some longer, more challenging stories in the issue. On page 88, Danielle Campoamor writes about raising a child to love their body if you struggle to love your own, and on page 46 Jennifer Chen reports on the damaging silence that persists around miscarriages. If this is your first time reading *Kindling,* you might be surprised to find these stories sharing space with the goofier things. But raising a child encompasses both utter silliness and profound challenges. We want this magazine to run the gamut of emotions alongside you.

One of the best parts of launching *Kindling* has been getting to know our new readers. We'd like to extend a huge thanks to the people who have sent ideas, shared the magazine with friends, or replied to our Community Questions on Instagram at @kindlingmagazine. Lastly, a statistically unlikely number of our contributors have welcomed babies between the start and end of us making this issue, including both our design director Alex and advertising manager Jessica. Congratulations on your new families!

Editor in Chief
HARRIET FITCH LITTLE

COMMUNITY QUESTION

"Sleep was called *Shoo Shoo* after the vintage cartoon snoring sound." (Mindy, USA)

SHOO SHOO

"My son hates it when we disagree, so to take the edge off it we call it *Baking Banana Bread*. He'll yell 'Don't bake banana bread please!' and then we'll all laugh." (Imke, The Netherlands)

BAKING BANANA BREAD

"Mom once couldn't remember the word for something and called it the hoover, so now we use *Hoover* whenever we can't think of the word we need." (Chloe, Guernsey)

HOOVER

"If you want to give someone a little tickle you have to say *Jib Jub* while doing it. If it's a longer tickle you can say *Jib Juuuuuub*. It's something my stepdad started doing when he'd tickle the cat." (Freddie, UK)

JIB JUB

"We use *Acariñar* a lot. In Mexico *acari-ciar* means caress and *cariño* means cuddle." (Patricia, Mexico)

ACARIÑAR

"From time to time, my kids like to throw every soft item in the house into one big pile and create a *Snountain* (snuggle mountain)." (Lindsay, USA)

SNOUNTAIN

What are the weirdest words in your "familect"?

Thanks to everyone on Instagram who replied to this prompt! Follow @kindlingmagazine to see more weird and wonderful answers. SEE MORE ONLINE!

"*Fififen* means the biggest number ever. My six-year-old tells us she love us 'a fififen'." (Camille, Netherlands)

FIFIFEN

"As a kid I called my bottle a *Wee-Wack*. My mom would often try and bribe me with the promise of a chocolate wee-wack." (Alex, *Kindling* design director)

WEE-WACK

"My family euphemistically refers to money sent in a card as a *Paperclip*. I was in my mid-twenties and still telling people I'd been sent a paperclip for my birthday. Everyone must have felt quite sorry for me." (Harriet, *Kindling* editor in chief)

PAPERCLIP

"Instead of saying *escargot* (snail), our daughter says *Chicago*. When we're out and about it's Chicago here, Chicago there." (Lydia, France)

CHICAGO

"*Binty* means blanket. I remember my dad talking to some movers asking them to 'put a binty' on some furniture, and they were so confused." (Heather, USA)

BINTY

Tita Tita means clock, based on my son's pronunciation of the clock sound." (Adam, Slovakia)

TITA TITA

Part 1:
FIRST STEPS

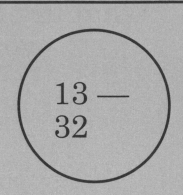

13 —
32

KIDS' CORNER:
Learn how to make
a hi-vis sash on
page 45 and how to
decorate a crutch
on page 87.

Part 2:
BIG READS

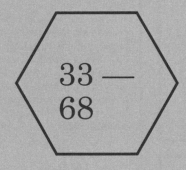

33 —
68

"Being with young children really
            changes your picture of the world."

P.67 — Alison Gopnik

On page 70, we've teamed up with hit podcast *Wow in the World* to answer kids' curious questions about their bodies.

69 — 108

Part 3:

THE BODY

Part 4:

FUN STUFF

Looking for a quick fix? Turn to page 110 for five fun games to occupy five minutes.

Born in 1949. Thousands of new combinations yet to be discovered.

≡string

Movie set designer Miriam Myrtell's combination. Discovered in 2021.

First Steps

13 — 32

When my now two-year-old son started daycare last year, I quickly discovered that pick up time was not the place where I'd learn about his mood, naps and dietary quirks of the day—particularly in the age of COVID-19. Like a growing number of facilities, his daycare now keeps me abreast of his progress on its app rather than its doorstep.

These apps—which have names like Famly, Tapestry, HiMama and brightwheel— are closed social media platforms, little LinkedIns for babies. They allow daycares to share announcements that are relevant for every child— requests to bring in sunscreen, for example—but also tailored information about a particular child: what they ate today and how much, what times they got their diaper changed, how long they napped for. You also get sent cute pics of your child at play, and information that puts their development in context.

I like using the app. When I log in and see my son has eaten all of his lunch, I get the same sort of low-level dopamine rush I do when I log into social media and see that I've accrued a lot of likes. I also marvel at the alternative life he leads in my phone. So, he's "leading them by the hand" to the changing table when he's pooped now? Did someone switch him for a different child? And how did staff manage to get him to eat "veggie stroganoff"? Sometimes, if I miss him, I can click on the app and sense his presence by scrolling through the abstract log of his activities. In fact, I find myself wishing it were available on the days when he gets looked after by his granny instead.

But I also worry about what the app has done to my experience of parenthood. When he's at nursery, my son's app-self is always with me in my pocket. I must remind myself that it isn't really "him": this child whose activities are logged as mere happenings, whose development is understood only in relation to a set of abstract general criteria. My son's app-self is a reliable report of his basic functions: that he naps when he's supposed to and eats all his toast. But this is not the child who gives me a big, soft hug at the door when I leave, or points and waves at all the buses as we walk back home. *That* child is in his bubble with his little friends, running around and giggling and covering himself in paint and getting in trouble for pushing.

I suppose, in this sense, daycare apps are dogged by the same problem of all social media: they're used to present some idealized version of the self. What's really important about my son's life at daycare isn't happening on the app, but beyond it.**k**

Updates from carers are particularly important when a child is pre-verbal. But even the most chatty older child can be reluctant to share what they got up to in class. Turn to page 24 for some tips to get them talking.

Words
TOM WHYMAN

— **Big Brother**
From drop-off chats to daycare apps.

The holiday letter is as entrenched a festive tradition as turkey. If well judged, these missives can be a charming window into other families' lives that double as helpful reminders of the names and ages of friends' children. But the letters, like the turkey, are often overcooked. They tend to be festivals of bragging rendered in florid prose. Report cards, endearing anecdotes and exotic holidays jostle for attention in Times New Roman. Divorces and redundancies get less of a look in.

Over the years, my family has built up a healthy subscription list. The first thing I do when I go home for the December holidays in London is pan through the correspondence for gold. I've found Americans, by nature more effusive, have a broader range than the British. I've read 1,000 words of direct evangelism. Letters from the point of view of the dog. One memorable example gave thanks that, in George W. Bush, the Lord had provided a president with the strength and judgment to lead the world through crisis.

The other side of the coin, which I try to forget, is that I know my parents write their own. Sometimes I fantasize about how they would cover me if I weren't so dull. "Ed (34) is serving six months for fraud. He's always had a naughty streak!" "Ed (34) has eloped to warmer climes with his personal trainer (18). Good luck!" "Ed (34) has been canceled (again)! Bad luck!"

I may not have to worry for long. The boomers have migrated to Facebook, where they can keep friends and family abreast of things 24/7. My fellow millennials and I have Instagram and Twitter. The kids boast on TikTok. The next lot will have something else. I'll be sad to see the letters go. As tin-eared as they can be, they come from an essentially good place: the desire to keep in touch. You don't know what you've got until it's gone—unless, of course, you had the foresight to write it down and mail it out to everyone you know. **k**

'Tis the season to be boastful.

— The Holiday Letter

Words
ED CUMMING

Guidance for secular guides.

— The Godparent

Words
JUSTIN MYERS

Godparents are
an example of
chosen family.
In many cultures,
terms such as
"auntie" or
"cousin" are used
to denote this
form of kinship.

To be a godparent is a divine duty within certain Christian denominations. Depending on the particulars of one's faith, the job might entail looking smart and serious at a baptism, renouncing the devil or pledging to be a lifelong moral guardian. But many more people now have godchildren than attend baptisms: It is a concept that has fled the nest of the faithful. Relieved of spiritual obligations, is the job anything more than a vanity title?

In the first instance, any godparent is a vital sympathetic shoulder to shell-shocked new parents, a wiper of goo from adorable chins or an on-call babysitter. They say it takes a village to raise a child, but with families often living far apart, godparents stand in for distant aunties or uncles. These connections can prove as strong as family, especially in the formative years.

As my own godchildren grew up, I learned that useful godparents are also mediators: I became the United Nations in unthreatening leisurewear, gravitating toward adult or child depending on who needed me most in their corner.

A godparent's choice word carries more gravitas than the usual telling-off, but sometimes you'll side with the godchildren, truly coming into your own during arguments over homework or untidy bedrooms. (My tip: Always speak to even very young children in the same voice you use for everyone else; baby talk is patronizing and easily tuned out.) As a sounding board, voice of reason or key witness, your biological or emotional distance from the family can help bring everyone closer together.

But perhaps your most useful role long-term is humanizing your friend, giving them, and their actions, context. Your relationship shows the child that the person raising them isn't just an irritable nag; they're a real, complex person, with pasts lived, countless mistakes made and lessons learned. That shared history binds you. Since the death of my godsons' mother, my best friend, just as I see so much of her in them, they too can find comforting traces of her within me. There's a lifetime of trust there for the taking; the strength of that bond depends on you. **k**

WI-FI ON WHEELS

Wi-Fi buses were deployed in several US counties during the pandemic to try and reach 3,700,000 households without consistent internet access. The signal, which reaches approximately 300 feet, enabled some children to work from home and others from cars or while sitting outside close to the bus.

OFFLINE LEARNING

Two-thirds of the world's school-age children don't have internet in their homes. In the US alone, roughly 30% of all public school students live in households without either an internet connection or a device adequate for distance learning, or both. Around the globe, viral stories have emerged of the lengths children are going to in order to access Wi-Fi: In Iran, a young boy was injured falling on a mountain that he climbed to access better signal in order to join an online class, while in Brazil a boy used a shopping mall tablet to complete his homework.

LUXURY OR UTILITY?

In 2019, 80% of US adults agreed that it was the government's responsibility to provide high-quality K-12 education for children. At the same time, only 28% said that the federal government had a responsibil-ity to provide high-speed internet access to the country. Now that the former is often dependent on the latter, those numbers are changing: By April 2021, the percentage of people citing the internet as a fundamental re-sponsibility had jumped to 43%.

— The Digital Divide
The other side of screen time.

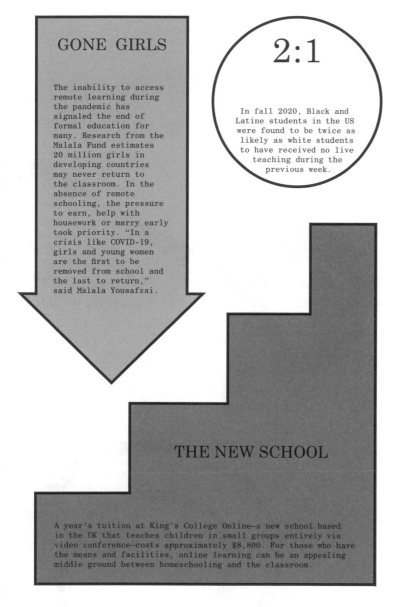

GONE GIRLS

The inability to access remote learning during the pandemic has signaled the end of formal education for many. Research from the Malala Fund estimates 20 million girls in developing countries may never return to the classroom. In the absence of remote schooling, the pressure to earn, help with housework or marry early took priority. "In a crisis like COVID-19, girls and young women are the first to be removed from school and the last to return," said Malala Yousafzai.

2:1

In fall 2020, Black and Latine students in the US were found to be twice as likely as white students to have received no live teaching during the previous week.

THE NEW SCHOOL

A year's tuition at King's College Online—a new school based in the UK that teaches children in small groups entirely via video conference—costs approximately $8,800. For those who have the means and facilities, online learning can be an appealing middle ground between homeschooling and the classroom.

At the height of COVID-19 -related closures in April 2020, 90% of all school-age students around the world had their education disrupted. The scourge of "screen time" gained new significance when it became the main channel through which lessons in algebra, science and (somehow) gym were delivered. But while some families were able to set children up in private study spaces with multiple devices, others were sharing a single screen with siblings, connecting over a smartphone or not connecting at all. In September 2020, UNICEF estimated that over half of the 872 million students who were still locked out of the classroom had not been reached by any form of distance learning. **k**

Turn to page 119 for a list of our sources.

$789.49

The projected spending per US family (with school-age children) for the start of the 2020 school year. The record price tag was the result of needing to buy electronics and desks for at-home learning.

"AROUND THE GLOBE, VIRAL STORIES
HAVE EMERGED OF THE LENGTHS CHILDREN ARE GOING
TO IN ORDER TO ACCESS WI-FI."

Words
ANDY MORRIS

— On The Couch
In defense of Daddy Pig.

Fatherhood is more flippant on screen. Sitcom dads tend to be either lazy, beer-guzzling lumps (Homer Simpson, Peter Griffin, Al Bundy) or exasperated workaholics (Bob Belcher, Johnny Rose, Uncle Phil).

On preschool TV shows, the parameters are broadly similar, but with a twist. Because writers are reluctant to show truly bad behavior or marital disharmony—which is, after all, the lifeblood of the sitcom family setup—fathers in several shows for toddlers are notable mainly for their absence. Our pint-sized heroes are often raised by saintly moms or surrogates, such as huggable labrador Duggee.

But there is at least one father figure who breaks the mold: Daddy Pig. He is perhaps the true hero of *Peppa Pig*, a British phenomenon with over 300 episodes, broadcast in 180 countries and worth over $1 billion. Each five-minute episode focuses on Peppa, George, Mummy and Daddy tackling some minor irritant: a messy room, a noisy sleepover. With the consistency so prized by the preschool demographic, each saga ends with the whole family rolling around on the floor snorting and laughing.

On first watch, Daddy Pig appears to be your run of the mill boastful fool. But "first watch" is a distant memory for a parent of two Peppa-obsessed children: I have watched all 27 available hours of piggy peril multiple times. On the third run-through, or perhaps it was the fourth, I was struck by a shocking realization: Is Daddy Pig actually a good template for fatherhood? Rather than the "silly daddy" that Peppa considers him to be, Daddy Pig is a doting porker who knows the secret to happiness is participating fully in his children's lives. As Peppa co-creator Neville Astley once told *Esquire*: "We all come up with our own examples of how useless we are. And the thing is, [Daddy Pig] is a bumbling fool, but then when it comes to it, he's also a tower of strength as well."

Daddy Pig may be a blundering bore, but he "isn't a complete idiot and buffoon. He turns it around," Astley insists. The piggy patriarch preps lunches, devises games on rainy days and is a regular at school events. On one occasion Daddy Pig even appears as a volunteer basketball coach, where he masterminds the kids' triumph over their parents and deftly sinks a shot of his own from the opposite end of the court. After meticulous comparative study of my pre- and post-bedtime viewing, I realize that there is one sitcom father who falls into the same category: *Modern Family*'s Phil Dunphy. On children's TV, the dad in Australian cartoon *Bluey* would also give Daddy Pig a run for his money.

This is not to say that Daddy Pig doesn't have his share of faults. Compared to the multi-hyphenate Miss Rabbit, he isn't that productive. His sexist dismissal of Mummy Pig's volunteering work as a firefighter nearly ends in disaster. But what Daddy Pig manages is to teach fathers to laugh at themselves. Rather than a caricature of the worst aspects of fatherhood, he is a parent who has defined what is truly important. He may only be "a bit of an expert," as the song goes, but I aspire to be as dedicated a dad. k

Daddy Pig's weight is a running joke, with Peppa and friends frequently poking fun at his "big belly." Turn to page 88 for an essay that explains why this is probably not a great approach for a children's program to take.

— **Sick Day Supplies**
Home comforts for
poorly people.

Brew your way back to health with a kettle from HAY.

Do the robot from your bed with the AREAWARE Cubebot.

Keep tingly toes cozy with socks from ENTIREWORLD.

Feel the (precise) heat with a WITHINGS thermometer.

Make duvet days feel divine with TEKLA bedding.

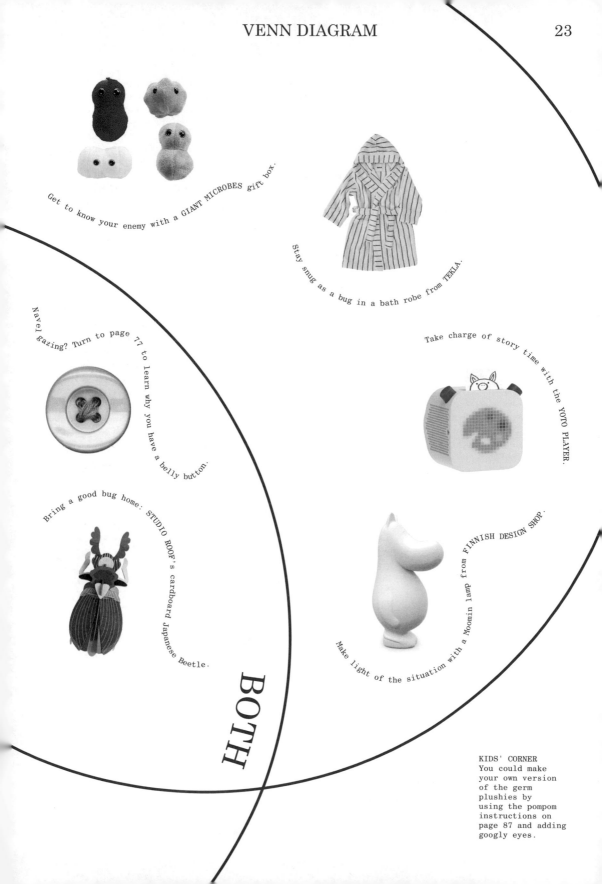

Get to know your enemy with a GIANT MICROBES gift box.

Stay snug as a bug in a bath robe from TEKLA.

Navel gazing? Turn to page 77 to learn why you have a belly button.

Take charge of story time with the YOTO PLAYER.

Bring a good bug home: STUDIO ROOF's cardboard Japanese Beetle.

Make light of the situation with a Moomin lamp from FINNISH DESIGN SHOP.

BOTH

KIDS' CORNER
You could make
your own version
of the germ
plushies by
using the pompom
instructions on
page 87 and adding
googly eyes.

Question
from an adult:

WHY DOES MY
CHILD SAY THEY
DID "NOTHING"
AT SCHOOL?

In the company of my normally gregarious children, there are a couple of simple questions that lead consistently to dead air. *What did you do today?* "Nothing." *What did you learn at school?* "I don't know."

Children of all ages can prove reluctant to speak about how they occupy their time away from you, although the reason varies. With younger children, the struggle is real; their ability to store memories and recall them chronologically is still developing. Questions about the shape of their day generally elicit routine answers: they snacked, played outside and ate lunch.

However, young children *can* respond to clues. It helps if you know some specifics about what they normally do so you can ask targeted questions. As always, be careful what you wish for: The question "What songs did you learn today?" once unlocked 20-plus minutes of singing from the backseat.

As children get older, their ability to recall unique events improves and they become more attuned to the social dynamics around them. But they develop other reasons to be tight-lipped. It is healthy for kids to want to hold some of their stories private. Don't interrogate them. You're not a detective harboring an uncooperative suspect—treating them as such will prompt silence or, worse, false confessions full of the answers they know you want to hear. If a child doesn't want to share, you can model what the conversation sounds like by telling them about your day. Tell them honestly about the moments you felt nervous or unsure.

Remember, it may simply be the case that your child can think of several more interesting things to talk about than school. Elementary age children enjoy philosophical conversations. If what you want is a discussion, rather than a diary entry, try engaging them with a wild hypothesis or an exercise in creative storytelling. "I wonder what it would be like if..." you can begin. They can take it from there. **k**

Words
JILL CEDER

— **Great Question!**
Smart answers to tricky queries.

Question from
a child:

WHY DOES
THAT PERSON
LOOK FUNNY?

Words
RUDRI BHATT
PATEL

A public outing with a young child can feel like an adventure safari; seeing the world through their ever-curious eyes can be invigorating and charming. But it can also be awkward. Curiosity is, by its very nature, undiscerning: The same child who delights you while grocery shopping by asking where pasta grows, and whether you can grow some too, may then lock eyes with a stranger browsing the tortellini and ask loudly: "Why does that person look funny?"

In public, "sometimes innocent curiosity wins," says Lesley Isaak, a Phoenix-based family counselor. Children will likely notice and comment on what is outside their norm, whether that's a woman with purple hair or a man with one arm. Adults can say, "Isn't it cool how people look so many different ways?" or "I love seeing all kinds of people. It makes our world so beautiful." If the person heard the comment, it is better to say your reply so they can hear you being proactive about the interaction. It also opens the door for them to directly address the child's question if they want to—a decision that is entirely up to them. "Try to avoid shushing or shaming your child. It will likely escalate the situation and cause further unintended insult," adds Isaak.

At home, emphasize to your child how to use discretion. "I love it when you share interesting things you're seeing! Please share them with me, instead of the whole room," suggests Isaak. To probe further, "find out what exactly is 'funny,' in your child's perception." Sometimes adults make assumptions and may address the wrong issue. Explore how the child feels about the "funny" person—are they concerning? Interesting? Cool?

Caregivers can normalize differences by reading books together or turning to diverse media that addresses these issues and having open conversations about differences that exist within your own family or community, whether that's grandma using a cane or a cousin who stutters. With time, they'll learn that "funny" is just a matter of perspective: there's no right way to be. **k**

Q&A:

MEQUITTA AHUJA's son was born in February 2019. Two weeks later, she learned that her mother was dying. Through her powerful self-portraiture, the artist probes this painful intersection — and everything that came after.

Born in 1976, Mequitta Ahuja received her BA in 1998 from Hampshire College in Amherst, MA, and her MFA in 2003 from the University of Illinois, during which time she was mentored by the artist Kerry James Marshall. The influences she draws from are as diverse as Poussin's 17th-century portraiture and the writing of Doris Lessing—from whom she absorbed the idea that it is important to show the interaction between a work of art and its genesis; a process Mequitta often represents by showing paintings within paintings. In December 2020, her exhibition *Ma* ran at New York's Aicon Gallery and featured works relating to her mother, who died in May 2020 from uterine cancer.

RPP: You exhibited *Ma* at New York's Aicon Gallery earlier this year. What have you been working on since?

MA: I've been merging my own features with my mother's features and trying to make the sort of mother and child image which is so much of the history of art; paintings of the mother and child that go back to the Virgin Mary. These works are still about, in a way, losing my mom as I was becoming a mother, but it's all distilled into this single mother/child image.

RPP: How is the work reflective of your relationship with your mother?

MA: I've been thinking about this kind of eternal feeling of being my mother's child. Even as she was aging and dying, I was still her baby. [Now], she's still my mom.

Her illness and death were so swift that we actually moved next door to my parents. I would see my mom every day, but I wasn't her caretaker. Obviously, I was going to do whatever my mother needed, but at the same time, I wanted to preserve our relationship. I remember calling her at one point and I was upset about something, and I wanted to say, in my usual way, "Mom, what do I do?" I remember saying to her that I wasn't sure how to be with her anymore. Do we just proceed as we always have or do we need to make a different kind of shift? Should I not be calling her with my

problems? She said, "I don't want our closeness to end just because I'm sick. That would be the worst thing that could happen; if our relationship lost a dimension of intimacy as a result of my illness." She gave me the freedom—permission— to maintain that dynamic.

RPP: Did you know of your mom's illness while you were pregnant?

"THESE DRAWINGS BECAME A DAILY PRACTICE OF GRIEVING."

MA: We had such a difficult time conceiving. We did IVF. It was just, like, epic. My baby is a miracle of science baby. But I had such an easy, happy pregnancy. My son was two and a half weeks old when we got her diagnosis.

RPP: You moved next door to your mother and eventually began working on paintings inspired by her. How did that work with a newborn in the house?

MA: I had to come up with a process where I could work quickly while my son was napping. I started doing oil sketches and making these fast, very loose gestural works where I put the paint down and

then scraped it off. It felt right to me as a process because it was creating something out of loss, out of taking something away. Even before she actually passed away, these drawings became a daily practice of grieving.

RPP: At what point did you show your mother what you were working on?

MA: It was pretty early on that I invited her over to see the oil sketches. She told me which one she liked, and we ended up hanging it next to her bed. My mom's not super demonstrative. She's a deep-feeling, passionate person, but she's pretty mellow. (I still use the present tense.) So she wasn't super emotive about it, but I think it meant a lot to her to know she inspired a body of work. And it meant a lot to me, to know that she knew that I was turning the experience into something lasting.

RPP: For the paintings that appeared in *Ma*, you used nude photos as source material—images that you and your mom had taken together while you were in graduate school. Tell me about the decision to use photos from the past, as opposed to more recent images.

MA: I didn't want to base my whole representation on this very short period when I was losing her. I don't know that it was a rational or conscious decision. And I didn't want to enlist her in any work while she was so ill.

Mequitta lives in a forested area of Connecticut and works out of a studio hidden from the road by trees. Although she spent much of her working life elsewhere—in Harlem, Houston, Chicago and Baltimore—she grew up in the area where she now lives and used to babysit for the family living in the house she now owns.

Nick, who
photographed
Mequitta, says
he was struck by
the extraordinary
scale of her
work and how she
breaks down light
and shadow into
vibrant colors.
In the paintings
shown here she
has combined
her own features
with those of
her mother.

"I WANT MY SON TO KNOW THAT SHE WANTED A RELATIONSHIP WITH HIM. THAT THEY WOULD HAVE BEEN CLOSE."

"I FEEL LIKE I GET TO DO IT ALL AGAIN, BUT THIS TIME I GET TO BE THE MOM."

One time I showed her the [old] photographs and the comment she made immediately was, "I miss my flesh." That's what she said. "I miss my flesh." So for her, that's the body she felt like her[self in].

My new drawings are sort of inspired by [photographs I took the week she died], even though they don't look like my mom, in the way that you can see a kind of skull in the face. The cancer completely devastated her desire and her physical ability to eat, so you could see the shape of her bone structure. Maybe it sounds perverse, but I was like, *that's interesting*. The body is fascinating. It was also disturbing. I'm an artist. That was part of what made it interesting—that it's so disturbing.

RPP: Though they had very little time together, what was your mother's relationship with your son like?

MA: My son was nursing or asleep in my lap, and she just looked at me and said, "You have a baby." I think we were both still in awe that it happened after all the work trying to conceive.

[Now] I tell him, "We miss Nani. Nani died." That was the hardest thing for my mom, actually. She said one thing that she regretted was that she wasn't going to see him grow up. I want him to know that she wanted a relationship with him. That they would have been close.

RPP: Do you ever feel like your mom is still near?

MA: I have had several dreams of my mother that felt so real that I wouldn't know how, or if, the mind distinguishes them from memories or actual events. At other times, I have had surreal dreams of my mom that were obviously symbolic of my profound loss and sadness. That the mind conjures such seemingly tangible and deeply felt experiences truly amazes me, and I am heartened to have learned that I can have new experiences of my mother. I wake up some mornings feeling as though I have just spent time with her.

RPP: How are you doing?

MA: Losing my mother has made parenting harder, but being a parent has made embracing a new life —a different life—easier. I feel like I get to do it all again, but this time, I get to be the mom. **k**

Photographer Nick says he envies the fact that Mequitta's son was happy to pose with her—unlike his own daughter.

"I decided I'd rather spend my life with the babies than the philosophers."

ALISON GOPNIK
PAGE 62

Big Reads

PHOTOGRAPHY: RODRIGO CARMUEGA

Play

Hi-vis and high fashion collide in our extremely loud and

Safe

incredibly bright kids shoot.

Below: Blue wears
a shirt and hat
by ARKET, neither
of which offers
much protection
in these (MARKS &
SPENCER) croc-
infested waters.
Opposite: Jacob
wears a sweater,
shorts and socks
from ARKET and a
hi-vis jacket
that our stylist
Ruth got from,
um, AMAZON.

Previous spread:
Jacob wears a
jacket by K-WAY,
shorts by PAGAIA
and boots by MARKS
& SPENCER. Blue
wears a T-shirt,
shirt and hat by
ARKET, trousers
by RALPH LAUREN
and crocs by
MARKS & SPENCER.
Both children are
wearing bags made
by Ruth using
hi-vis fabric.

Jacob wears a
T-shirt, shirt and
shorts by RALPH
LAUREN, an orange
sash made by Ruth
and a hi-vis jacket
from, you guessed
it, AMAZON.

Blue wears a
shirt and hat by
ARKET, trousers by
BURBERRY, boots by
MARKS & SPENCER and
a bag made by Ruth.

Fluorescent pre-adolescents! Look a million megawatts with bags, vests and hats that bring the spotlight with you.

Jacob wears a
jacket by K-WAY
and a bag made by
Ruth. He says his
favorite thing
about the shoot
was that he got to
wear "costumes"
rather than normal
clothes.

Blue wears a
T-shirt by UNIQLO
and a shirt and
hat by ARKET. His
favorite thing
about the shoot
was playing tag
with Jacob and
goofing around
with photographer
Rodrigo.

Jacob wears a
T-shirt by UNIQLO,
a jacket by JOHN
LEWIS and boots by
MARKS & SPENCER.
Photographer
Rodrigo reports
that energy levels
rarely dropped
below the point
pictured in
this shot.

Bikers and builders and bodyguards.

Blue wears a
T-shirt by UNIQLO,
trousers by
BURBERRY, a shirt
and hat by ARKET,
socks by OFF-
WHITE, shoes by
MARKS & SPENCER
and a bag by NIKE.
The shoot began
with him reading
books between
takes, and ended
with him and Jacob
zipping around the
studio so fast
that no one could
catch them.

Rail workers, refuse collectors, emergency responders —and you!

Jacob wears a shirt and shorts by RALPH LAUREN and boots by MARKS & SPENCER. You can make a two-strap version of the sash he's wearing using the instructions here!

Design
RUTH
HIGGIN-
BOTHAM

HOW TO...

1.

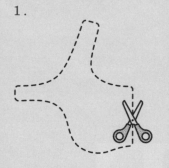

2.

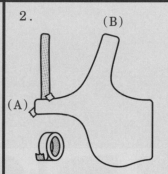

3.

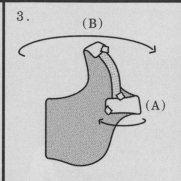

MAKE A VERSION OF RUTH'S HI-VIS SASH AT HOME.

4.

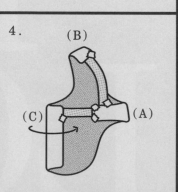

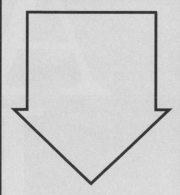

EQUIPMENT:
Hi-vis fabric
(or an old hi-vis gilet)
Scissors
Strap fabric
(or a couple of old straps)
Duct tape

1. Draw the shape pictured on the hi-vis side of your fabric. You can either draw it freehand or create a template on tracing paper and draw around that. The shape should be wide enough (left to right) to almost wrap around the body of the person wearing it. Cut the shape out using scissors.

2. Attach a strap to the left-hand fabric tab (A) using duct tape.

3. Turn the sash over. Fold the fabric tab with the strap attached (A) back in on itself, and then attach the other end of the strap to the shoulder tab (B) using another piece of duct tape.

4. Try your sash on! Once you've checked the sizing, join the sash together at the waist using another shorter strap (C) and secure it with more duct tape.

WORDS: JENNIFER CHEN

REPORT:

AFT ER LOSS

The grief of a miscarriage is often unspoken and the workplace provisions often non-existent. JENNIFER CHEN speaks to the people trying to change all that.

"We are not alone in our loss, but we often feel like we are the only ones going

In 2016, New Zealander Kathryn van Beek found out during a pregnancy scan that her baby was dying. She went home and cried all day. Van Beek, a writer, took four days of sick leave for her miscarriage, one of which was for surgery. As her statutory sick days dwindled, she researched New Zealand's Holidays Act and discovered that it allowed for bereavement leave if your child dies. Did that provision include her? "I thought it was important to clarify the wording so anyone who needed the leave could take it," Van Beek told me via email. She wrote to her local Member of Parliament, Clare Curran. Much to her surprise, Curran replied and took the cause to Parliament. Labour MP Ginny Andersen drafted the Bereavement Leave for Miscarriage Bill, which offers three paid bereavement days for people who have lost a pregnancy, their partners or those aiming to have a child through adoption or surrogacy. During her final reading of the bill, which was signed into law in March 2021, Andersen tweeted: "This is a Bill about workers' rights and fairness. I hope it gives people time to grieve and promotes greater openness about miscarriage. We should not be fearful of our bodies."

New Zealand isn't the first country to offer paid leave for a pregnancy loss. In fact, its three-day allowance is paltry compared to the handful of others with policies in place. India allows for six weeks leave following a miscarriage, although the law only applies to women who work at a company with 10 employees or more. The Philippines gives women 60 days of paid leave. Women in the Canadian province of Ontario who miscarry in the second half of their pregnancy can take 17 weeks of unpaid pregnancy leave. In the UK, the end of a pregnancy before 24 weeks doesn't qualify for bereavement leave, but a woman who has a stillborn after 24 weeks can take maternity leave.

In the United States, there are no federal laws in place for pregnancy loss leave. A few years ago, I suffered two miscarriages in California—one at 10 weeks and another at six weeks. After the first, I took two days off from work to recoup after a botched dilation and curettage. For the second loss, I took no time off. A few months after my first miscarriage, I wrote a personal essay for *BuzzFeed* about my experience of loss and grief. I was terrified to share such news openly, but I knew I wasn't alone. Hundreds of people reached out to me with their own stories.

Breaking the silence around miscarriage is an important step toward supporting families in their grief. Trystan Reese, a transgender man, lost his first pregnancy just shy of six weeks, an experience he shared on the parenting podcast, *The Longest Shortest Time.* "Even when I started to talk about my trans pregnancy story publicly, I was told, 'Do not talk about having a pregnancy loss,'" Reese tells me over Zoom. "Particularly through the trans lens, so much of what we hear is that it's already unnatural for us to have children."

But pregnancy loss is not uncommon or unnatural: One in four pregnancies ends in miscarriage. "Miscarriage is a strange kind of loss because it's so private, and that means it can be overlooked," Van Beek tells me.

The secrecy of the loss is interconnected with how we talk about pregnancy as a whole. Typically, people don't share their pregnancy news with friends and family until after the first trimester, usually around 12 weeks, after which the chances of miscarrying are significantly lower. There is a logic to this—it can be extremely painful to "retract" the news that a baby is coming from those most excited to hear it—but it also stems from the stigma that surrounds miscarrying. After my pregnancy loss, I was initially reluctant to speak about it for fear of judgement. But when I did tell two friends about what had happened, they in turn shared their experiences of miscarriage with me. We are not alone in our loss, but we often feel like we are the only ones going through it. Sharing our pregnancy stories—the good, the bad and the scary—not only opens the door to honest, vulnerable conversations, but also provides a realistic picture of the process.

In the workplace, there are also more practical considerations: People hide bumps or pregnancy symptoms because of the host of ways in which they fear pregnancy might disadvantage them. One study, from the UK's Equality and Human Right's Commission, found that around one in nine respondents had been dismissed or pushed out of jobs during pregnancy. For someone to feel safe talking about a miscarriage at work, they must first feel comfortable "outing" themselves as someone who is thinking about having children. "Workplaces and workplace cultures were initially built for men, and we are living in a time when women and non-binary people are advocating for ourselves and trying to make our workplaces work for us," says Van Beek

During a meeting with his boss, Reese burst into tears and disclosed his miscarriage months after the fact. He had never told his boss that he was trying to get pregnant so they had never talked about his loss. "I didn't know how to talk about it, especially as a transgender man... but feelings don't go away just because you don't talk about them," says Reese.

Now, as the CEO of Collaborate Consulting, Reese works with corporations and nonprofits to develop inclusive workplace policies. He believes that the language used for paid leave should be as inclusive as possible, and include all family members. To help families navigate their way through the grief of pregnancy loss, he recommends

through it. Sharing pregnancy stories opens the door to honest conversations."

"I convinced myself I had adequately addressed my loss in therapy. Then I wandered into the baby

companies offer workers flexible paid time off: "Let them take what is offered, and choose for themselves how to implement that time," he says.

Fleda Mask Jackson, an educator and the creator of Save 100 Babies, an organization based in Atlanta, Georgia, which is campaigning to reduce Black infant mortality, suggests companies consider their employees' overall health if they need a reason to take miscarriage provisions more seriously. "Depression, as the result of miscarriage, that is not addressed before a new pregnancy, has serious implications for birth outcomes and for the subsequent physical and emotional health of the mother and baby," she says. "Most people suffer in silence after the physical manifestations of miscarriage are addressed medically." These stresses are particularly acute for Black women, she says. "Stress from the lived experiences of racism and sexism, which is documented as a significant contributor to worse pregnancy, birth and maternal outcomes for Black American women, is likely a contributor to the higher rates of miscarriage that are recorded for African American women."

After my miscarriage, I convinced myself I had adequately addressed the loss in therapy. Then, during a shopping trip to Target with my husband, I wandered into the baby aisle. I can handle this, I thought, but as I perused rows of cute onesies and baby bottles, I felt my heart pound. Suddenly, I could feel the beginnings of a panic attack. I darted out of the aisle toward my husband. "I have to leave right now," I said. Grief pops up when we least expect it.

My hope is that as we collectively work toward a more equitable world and workplace, we don't have to endure in silence any more. After all, even the most well-thought-out miscarriage leave policies can only be used if a person is willing to talk about what they're going through. The Miscarriage Association, a UK-based organization, runs a website bursting with advice and useful precedents for employees and the self-employed: getting a doctor's note, managing a phased return to work, clarifying confidentiality. Among the pages of pragmatism one line of comfort stands out to me: "[People] may be more understanding than you think." **k**

Our writer Jennifer also spoke to Ginny Andersen, the Labour MP who drafted New Zealand's Bereavement Leave for Miscarriage Bill, for this feature. "Grief isn't a sickness, it's a loss, and loss takes time," Andersen told her. She recommends that private companies, when creating policies surrounding miscarriage, "leave it open enough that the person can lead what their recovery looks like, so they can do what's best for them."

We understand that this piece might be difficult or upsetting to read.
There are now several organizations that offer support for pregnancy loss including Share Pregnancy and Infant Loss Support in the USA and The Miscarriage Association in the UK. If you live elsewhere, both organizations have online communities or can point you toward support networks closer to home.

aisle in Target. I felt my heart pound. Suddenly, I could feel the beginnings of a panic attack. Grief pops up when we least expect it."

NOTES
ON CAMP:

Campfires, canoes... coding?
     This generation's summer camps
look very different to the last.

I THINK OF MYSELF as one of the lucky ones. For a stretch in my childhood, my parents packed my bags, wished me luck and shipped me off to summer camp. It was never for the whole summer—eight days at a Catholic-run girls camp deep in Muskoka cottage country; two weeks of YMCA-subsidized fun near Clear Lake, which more than lived up to its name—but the impressions have stuck. At 30, I can conjure the early morning flag-raisings and secular-ish mess hall "grace"; the crackle of birch bark in a fire pit and the smell of smoke in my braids; the cabin bunk beds with wipe-clean mattresses the thickness and softness of a King James Bible; bonding with girls from hometowns I'd never heard of and enjoying night after night of uninterrupted stars—so different from the view from my Toronto suburb.

To look at the sheer breadth of options available to campers today, the traditional sleepaway camp has never seemed so dated. Far from the campfires-and-canoes image of democratized outdoor leisure so many of us grew up on —fostered as much by life experience as by either version of *The Parent Trap*—today's modern camps look suspiciously like school. In glowing prospectus photos, smiling kids learn about coding and rudimentary robotics, study second and third languages and infiltrate laboratories at top universities. Is this camp, or are these expensive academic hothouses where the privileged spawn of helicopter parents grow their lead?

It's a question that educators, academics and camping professionals are increasingly contending with. "This is a thing that we argue about all the time on campus: When is camp not camp any longer, and when is it just an extension of school or academic development or professional advancement?" says Ryan J. Gagnon, an assistant professor of parks, recreation and tourism management at Clemson University in South Carolina.

But in reality, many of these programs don't so much disrupt notions of camp as expand on their initial conceit. The ideal of summer camp as a sacred site for fun, growth and communion with nature has always been something of a fiction, tinted at once with nostalgia and optimism. "Fun was always a central mandate of camps, definitely. But it was never the exclusive mandate," explains Leslie Paris, author of *Children's Nature: The Rise of the American Summer Camp*. "There was always a sheen of, 'This is going to be educational; this will be good for [children's] socialization; this will be good to develop them body and mind.'"

The image of camp that exists in the popular imagination dates to the late 19th century, as industrialization drew Americans of all classes— as well as new immigrants— into dense cities. At the time, parental concerns about what constituted a well-rounded summer education were decidedly different.

The earliest institutions, Paris explains, were spawned from the anxieties of middle-class, educated white men in Northeastern cities who worried about how urban living

"When is camp not camp, and when is it just an extension of school or academic development?"

Researching this story brought back lots of memories for writer Allyssia, including the time she decided to introduce herself at camp roll call as Ally, "who I imagined would be more fun and popular and less self-conscious and, shall we say, *niche* than Allyssia." The rebrand was surprisingly successful, and she became something of a camp Queen Bee for the summer. "Looking back, it obviously wasn't the nickname that got me out of my shell that summer, but the audacity and confidence," she says. "They've both served me well ever since."

would impact their sons in the long run. "They were concerned the boys of their class were going to become effete," she explains. "They weren't going to have outdoor, vigorous activities that challenged them to build a kind of muscular manhood that would let them become the elite men of the next generation."

In 1881, Dartmouth student Ernest Balch founded Camp Chocorua in New Hampshire—often cited as America's first children's summer camp—with a Thoreau-like zeal for the restorative power of nature. By that point, many urban centers had started introducing months-long summer breaks into the calendar (then, as now, the rich fled dense, poorly ventilated cities to escape summer heat) which made it the perfect season to squeeze in life lessons between academic grades. At his camp, Balch corralled well-to-do campers into swimming, canoeing, water sports, baseball and other traditions that have become synonymous with camp and "character building." This spirit of soft education would persist as camps grew in popularity and were embraced by caregivers and children alike across all demographics.

But the mission was never just about building character:

"It's like an arms race... It's awful to think that we're excluding a whole group of kids."

At Camp Chocorua, for example, Balch made the instilling of entrepreneurial skills a big part of his mission. "There were some camp directors who gave lectures in natural history to their campers and some who offered tutoring in the summer," Paris says. "There was always a kind of hybridity."

Skills-based specialty summer camps like the ones we see now aren't unprecedented either. People have been sending their children to academically inclined summer camps since the 1960s, when Congress backed the creation of "Science Island"—a residential camp off the coast of Maine with a mission to provide America's "most able youngsters" with "opportunity, guidance, and inspiration to become worthy and dedicated scientists."

In the 1970s, as an economic recession, cheap international travel, and the post-Baby Boom dip in demographics forced many traditional camps to close, speciality camps became a booming industry—so much so that athletics organizations such as World Championship Tennis (a precursor to the Association of Tennis Professionals) and the NBA union, as well as sporting legends Pelé and Joe Namath, opened their own camps to capitalize on the trend. Computer camps, meanwhile, go back nearly as far as home computing itself: By 1983, six years after the first computer camp was founded by an engineering professor at Fairfield University in Connecticut, the American Camping Association had 120 accredited camps that offered computer programs.

Just as the rarefied offerings have evolved, so too have attitudes about the purpose of camp. "There certainly has been rising anxiety in recent decades among many middle-class parents about whether their kids will achieve the same standard of living that they have, and concern about how to give them opportunities to succeed," says Paris.

Gagnon agrees: "It's like an arms race almost, if everyone is going to coding camp then Ryan and Allyssia [are] not going to get into that computer science program because we don't have the coding background that all of our peers do. It's awful to think that we're excluding a whole group of kids that might not have the financial ability to get [into one of these camps], or they might just not have the interest yet."

However, Gagnon points out, these academically-inclined camps can also level the playing field, particularly when it comes to camps that target communities typically underrepresented in sciences, technology, engineering and mathematics, such as women and people of color. "STEM camps offer a safer context to fail up and learn experientially," Gagnon explains. "These camps offer a mechanism... to show other people [how to make] their way into this realm that's traditionally dominated by white dudes."

Such was the intention behind Black Girls CODE, the San Francisco-based non-profit that has provided tech education to girls of color across America since 2011. "What's most unique about the summer programming at Black Girls CODE is that it has been customized specifically for black girl demographics. [The curriculum] connects not only with the values that we uphold, or how we'd like this generation to evolve, but also in terms of the hope that we hold for them to help advance the technology industry," says Kimberly Hollins, BGC's curriculum and education manager. "In our environments, I've seen quotes and surveys of young black girls saying, 'Wow, I've never seen so many girls like me,' and that in and of itself speaks to the need to center their identity in the tech sector."

Ultimately, the camping sector reflects the ever-shifting priorities and anxieties of parents and caregivers, and the looming demands of the adult world. People have always wanted what's best for their kids, but the bar is constantly changing.

"If you're running a camp, your customers are the parents, and as a parent, you want to know if your kid is better and different because of this experience," Gagnon says. "As Barry A. Garst, one of my very best colleagues, says, 'You fund what you value, and you value what you fund.'"

What those values *are* changes not only from generation to generation, but also from family to family and child to child. But the defining value of camp has less to do with the lessons kids are taught than the things they learn about themselves from the experience. I probably couldn't tell you the proper way to maneuver a kayak, but camp was never really about that. What called me back year after year—and not just to traditional camps, but also French camp and musical theater camp—was the thrill of escape and independence. Away from the familiar, camp offered the freedom to be my authentic self; it was a safe place to take risks, and the chance of finding a tribe I couldn't find at home. Camp is for kids, but it's where I grew up.

In 15 years, the kids building balsa wood bridges on college campuses will probably tell you the same thing. The curriculum may change, but the core lessons are the same. **k**

"If you're running a camp, your customers are the parents."

Work hard? Play hard!
The developmental psychologist
on what adults can
learn from babies.

go
pik

Alison Gopnik, a professor of psychology and philosophy at the University of California, Berkeley, has made many startling discoveries about how babies and young children think. They understand statistics and statistical patterns, for one. In many ways, they're better learners than us, their little brains nimbler and more sponge-like. And their pretend play, as seemingly chaotic and inexplicable as it may appear to grownups (and maddening, for those of us who clean up after them), is key to fostering their imaginations and creativity.

Much of her research flies in the face of previously held beliefs. "The great psychologist William James thought that babies lived in a blooming, buzzing confusion," she says. "The great philosopher John Locke thought that the baby's mind was a blank slate. Even the great developmental psychologist Jean Piaget thought that babies and young children were egocentric and solipsistic, and that they couldn't think very well. And I think a lot of people still think that to this day."

Gopnik clearly does not, and has combined research she's conducted in labs and childcare settings with her own experiences as a mother and grandmother to find out what's really going on inside the minds of the very young. She's also written several celebrated books about the subject, including *The Philosophical Baby: What Children's Minds Tell Us About Truth, Love, and the Meaning of Life,* and her latest, *The Gardener and the Carpenter: What the New Science of Child Development Tells Us About the Relationship Between Parents and Children.* In 2021, Gopnik received a coveted Guggenheim fellowship; the same year, she was awarded a lifetime achievement award from The Association for Psychological Science.

Photographer Cayce met Alison at her home in Berkeley, where she had a house busy with family visiting from Canada.

Today, Gopnik is in her Berkeley home, recalling her own upbringing. "I had a wonderful, strange, eccentric childhood," she says. Born and raised in Philadelphia, Gopnik and her five younger siblings grew up in a home filled with art, literature and music. She recalls a trip in the family's Volkswagen Bug, at age five, dressed in clothes sewed by her mom, to the opening of the Guggenheim Museum; at 10, she was acting in Bertolt Brecht's *Galileo*, in a production directed by the avant-garde director André Gregory (My Dinner with *André*).

"Being a parent is about forging a relationship with this individual person, one that will let them go out and discover the world."

She read Plato's *Dialogues* age 11, inspired by an adaptation of a play about Socrates she had just seen on TV. Riveted by the show, she also created her own Acropolis in her family's backyard, with sticks and stones standing in for arguing philosophers. "I thought that this activity that these people were engaged in, which was just, you know, thinking and talking, was the best thing I'd ever heard of," she says.

When she was 13, her family moved to Montreal. Two years later, Gopnik enrolled as a philosophy major at McGill University but ended up taking so many classes in psychology, another subject she was enthralled by, that she received degrees in both subjects. She went to Oxford for her Ph.D., where she finally had to choose between her two academic loves. Did she want to hang out on Oxford's fabled Logic Lanc with the philosophers, or at the other end of the campus, with the psychologists, studying kids? "I decided I'd rather spend my life with the babies than the philosophers," she says.

Gopnik began doing her research in earnest in the mid-1970s, at a time when there was an enormous revolution in how developmental psychologists were looking at babies and young children. Rather than being somehow defective or incomplete grownups, she discovered, young children actually have very different ways of learning

The Philosophical Baby, first published in 1998, presented groundbreaking scientific research to make the case that babies have a lot to teach us about what it means to be human.

KIDS' CORNER
See if you
can make a
sculpture as
big as the one
Alison has on
her bookshelf
by using the
method on
page 112!

than adults, ways that make their minds much more fluid and flexible. Take problem solving. Kids will look at a problem from dozens of different angles, trying out lots of things that probably won't work to figure out just what might. Grownups are much more deliberate and focused. So, while grownups might reach a solution more quickly, they often miss out on the sorts of creative learning that kids experience.

Can adults benefit from this more childlike approach in their own thinking? "Yes, there are lots of ways," says Gopnik. "And a lot of them involve putting yourself back in the same kind of position that children are in. You can try to master a new skill, like learning to play the cello in your 70s, which is something one of my friends has done. Even just sitting in the garden and breathing deeply and not doing anything for half an hour can help put you back in a more creative, more plastic state."

In her latest book, *The Gardener and the Carpenter,* Gopnik distinguishes between two very distinct parenting styles (in fact, Gopnik hates the use of "parenting" as a verb, as if it were work. She much prefers to see what we do as parents or caregivers or grandparents as simply "care," or "love"). Carpenter parents try to shape their kids as a woodworker might shape a kitchen table, sawing and sanding till you get what you want. They're the ones who tell their kids how and what to study, even how and what to play. Gardeners, on the other hand, create a safe and nurturing space for kids to learn and grow on their own. Ideally, you have a whole community of gardeners looking after your kids—from family friends to older siblings to grandparents—all teaching and loving them in different ways.

"I think parents nowadays tend to have this very instrumental picture about their relationship with children," Gopnik says. "They feel they have to do a whole bunch of things in order to make the child come out a particular way. And I don't think that's the right model for what being a parent is about. Being a parent is about forging a relationship with this individual person, [one] that will let that person go out and discover the world for themselves."

Her ideas about being a parent are informed by years of research observing and interacting with kids at childcare facilities, children's museums and at Berkeley's Child Study Center. But she also draws from her many and varied personal experiences as a mother of three and

In the summer of 2021, Alison was awarded the Carl Sagan Prize for Science Popularization.

Alison's mother was a woodworker and designed many objects in the home— including the desk that her books rest on.

a grandmother of four. One of her grandkids, Thalo, a "beautiful 10-month-old grandson," is with her in California right now, visiting with family after a year and a half away. "That separation because of COVID really made me realize how rich that experience of being with young children is, and how much it really changes your picture of the world," she says.

Gopnik is currently working on a variety of projects, including writing about a study on the effects of poverty and stress on brain development for *The Wall Street Journal*, and conducting research with artificial intelligence experts on the advantages of childlike play, for both kids and bots. It's all still fun for her, she says, certainly more so than if she had been swayed by the philosophers of Oxford's Logic Lane, and certainly more fun than other research she might be doing in Berkeley's psychology department. "Most cognitive psychologists are sitting there and giving grownup undergraduates reaction time experiments," she says. "What I get to do is so much more fun and more interesting. Because the kids almost always do things that are totally unexpected, that we wouldn't have thought that they would do. From a scientific perspective, it's just this constant ability to have surprises, to find out things that you wouldn't have thought of before." **k**

Alison told photographer Cayce that one of the reasons she knew her husband (the computer scientist Alvy Ray Smith) was a good match was how well their belongings fit together.

69 — 108

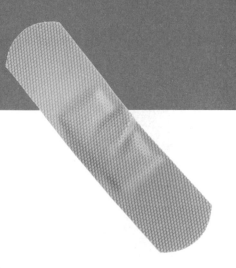

The Body

funny

Heads, shoulders,
knees and...
what are those?!

Wow in the World's Mindy Thomas answers kids' curious questions about the body.

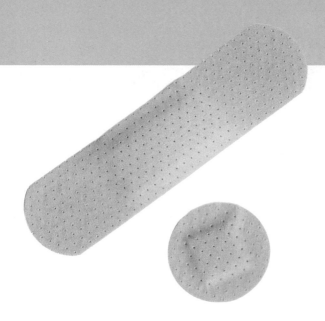

Q. How do vaccinations work?

Chances are, you've been hearing the word "vaccine" a lot lately. A vaccine is just a fancy word for what you may call a "shot." By now, you've probably received more than a few of them!

Vaccines introduce your immune system to certain germs so that your body can build up its army of germ-fighting antibodies. Should these germs make their way past your body's first lines of defense (tears, mucus, saliva, earwax, skin, blood and the stomach), the antibodies will instantly recognize what they're up against and storm into battle, destroying these germs and stripping them of their mutating powers! So the next time you feel the pinch of a vaccine needle, know that you're helping your immune system build up its defense for your body's next battle so you don't get sick.

Q. Why do I have to sleep?

We get it. You've got things to explore, snacks to eat, new people to meet and only 24 hours in a day. You don't have time for sleep. But what if you looked at sleep as a mini vacation that you give your body every single night? Your body gets to rest, relax and recharge for a brand new day tomorrow. And while your body is chilling, your brain is getting to work organizing everything you put into it while you were awake. It's sorting memories, storing information and even solving problems. Without sleep, your mind might become as messy as your room!

There is little evidence to support the common advice that counting sheep helps you fall asleep. In a 2001 study by researchers at Oxford University, it was found that insomniacs who counted sheep took longer to fall asleep than those who didn't.

Q. Why do adults have wrinkles?

Skin! It's a squishy, stretchy, waterproof raincoat for your guts. It's also the largest organ of your entire body. So what happens to it as we age? Well first, we should talk about the three layers that make up our skin. The top layer, and the only layer we can see, is called the epidermis. Underneath the epidermis is the layer we call the dermis. This is the layer from where hair and sweat make their way onto your body. The dermis is also home to teeny tiny fibers called elastins that allow our skin to stretch and then bounce back into place. The third and deepest layer is the hypodermis or subcutaneous layer. This is the layer that stores fat, providing soft padding for your muscles and bones. Over time, our skin starts to lose fat, elastin and oils, causing our skin to become thinner, drier and less stretchy as we age. The sun's ultraviolet rays have the power to speed up this process as they break down the fibers that make all of our stretchy elastin. All of this combined causes the wrinkles you may see on adults' skin, and one day on your own. This is all perfectly natural, and just another sign of growing up.

Q. Where does skin get its color from?

The color of your skin is determined by the amount of melanin you have in it. Melanin is a natural pigment, or color, and it affects the eye, hair and skin color of all humans. The more melanin in your body, the darker your skin; the less melanin in your body, the lighter your skin. Freckles and moles appear in spots with lots of extra melanin in the skin. Newborn babies don't have freckles because they haven't been exposed to the sun long enough for them to develop.

Melanin is also the reason that people with lighter skin get a tan when exposed to the sun. The sun's rays are harmful to our skin, so the body kicks in and produces more melanin to protect against it. But the best protection is sunscreen!

Q. What's the difference between a fart and a burp?

When you eat, you're swallowing more than just your food. With every bite, you're also ingesting air—and that air contains gas. As this food and gas work their way through your digestive system, they're broken down in your large intestine, where they make even more gas. Your body can't possibly contain it all, so it's got to find an escape route. Gases escaping from your butt are called farts, or, scientifically speaking, flatus. The average healthy person farts between 14 and 20 times a day. Like a fart, a burp is caused by swallowing air that contains gases when we eat or drink. But unlike a fart, a burp never makes its way to the large intestine. Instead, it's pushed out of the stomach, up through the esophagus, and out the mouth.

Q. Why do I have a belly button?

A belly button is just a scar left over from where your umbilical cord once was. You might be cordless now, but back in the day, when you were growing inside your birth parent's womb, your umbilical cord was how they were able to send oxygen and nutrients from their body to yours and you used it to send them back all the waste your growing body didn't need. Once you were born, it basically just fell off. Your body didn't need it any more.

Q. Is everyone born a boy or a girl?

Not all babies are born boys or girls, males or females. There are actually many more ways of being a person than most people realize. For example, some people are born with reproductive parts that don't necessarily match the specific characteristics of "male" or "female." Others, as they grow, may find that they don't identify with the "boy" or "girl" label they were given the day they were born. It's important to remember that the human race is a variety pack of nearly eight billion people, and no two are exactly alike.

Liz Kleinrock, an educator who is part of our editorial board, recommends two children's books on the topic of gender: *When Aidan Became a Brother* and *It Feels Good to Be Yourself*.

Q. Why can't I tickle myself?

Have you ever attempted to tickle yourself? Didn't work, did it? Scientists at the University of Cambridge think it may have to do with your cerebellum, the part of your brain that anticipates what different things feel like. When you tickle yourself, your cerebellum knows what to expect and isn't impressed. But when someone else tickles you… where did that come from?! In short, some scientists believe that the reason it's impossible to tickle yourself is because you can't surprise yourself.

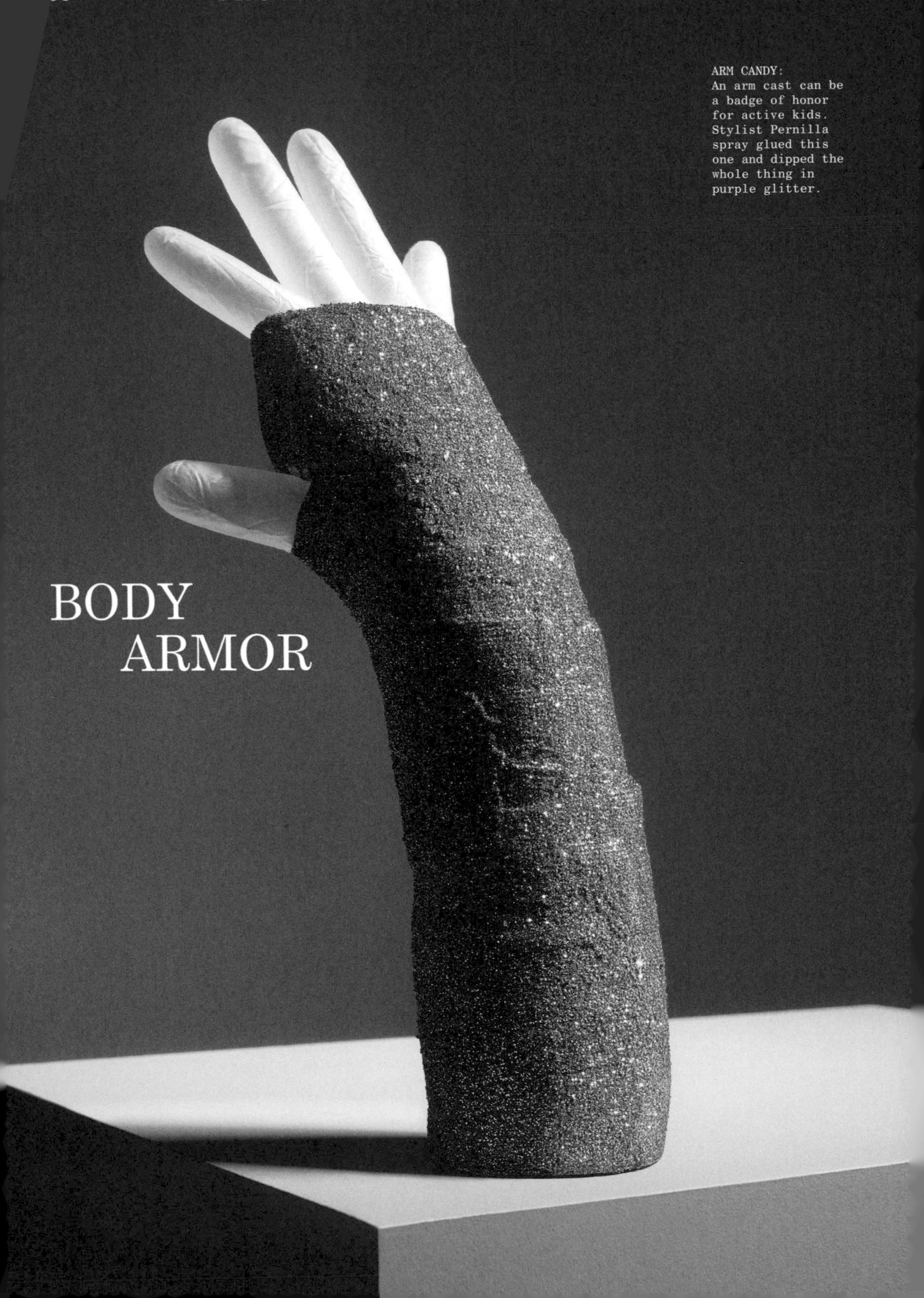

ARM CANDY:
An arm cast can be
a badge of honor
for active kids.
Stylist Pernilla
spray glued this
one and dipped the
whole thing in
purple glitter.

BODY
ARMOR

A spangled celebration of
the things that help our bodies
keep moving.

WHEELY BEAUTIFUL:
There is not a
single part of
this wheelchair
that isn't covered
with glitter.
Pernilla took the
whole thing apart
and sprayed each
component with
glitter paint
before carefully
putting it back
together again.

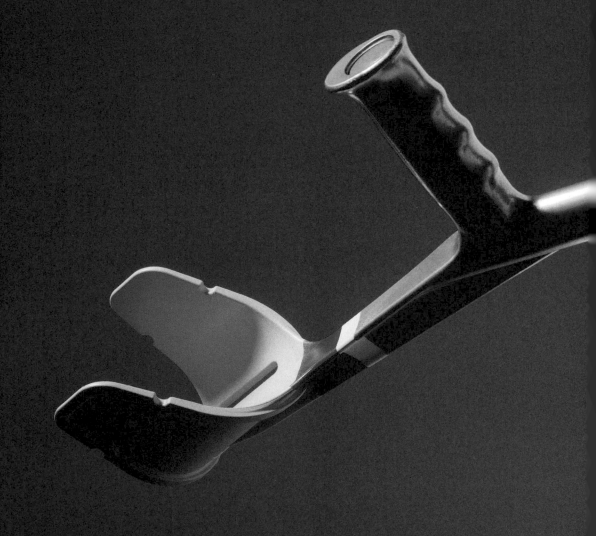

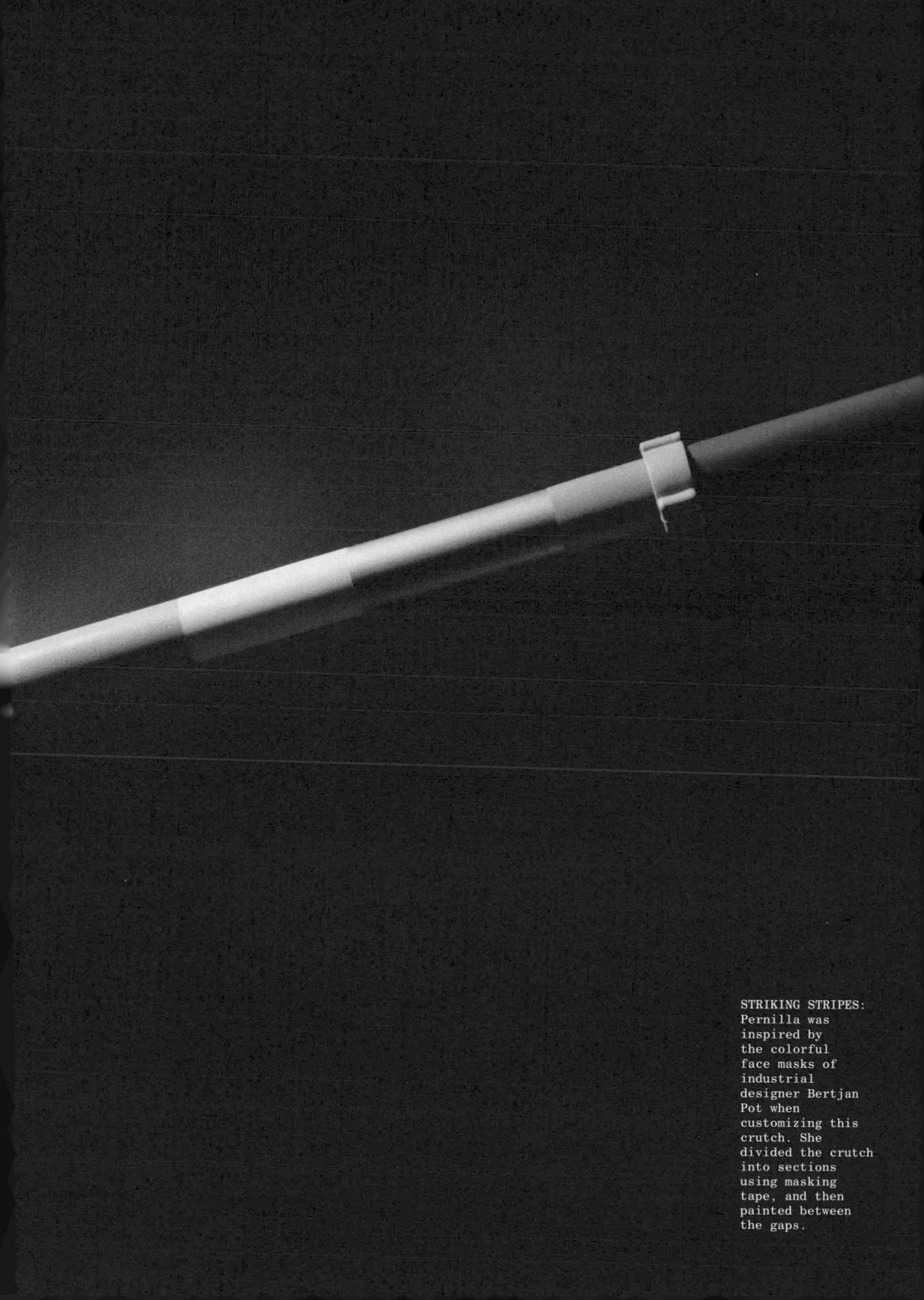

STRIKING STRIPES:
Pernilla was
inspired by
the colorful
face masks of
industrial
designer Bertjan
Pot when
customizing this
crutch. She
divided the crutch
into sections
using masking
tape, and then
painted between
the gaps.

LUCKY CHARM:
Pernilla's
"bedazzled and
over-the-top" take
on the Evil Eye—
an ancient symbol
of protection
in the eastern
Mediterranean and
some Middle Eastern
countries—uses
spray glitter,
plastic gems and
fake rhinestones.

ALL-STAR CAST:
"More is more,"
says Pernilla about
her leg cast. It's
a celebration of
the fun that can
be had with a
well-stocked craft
drawer and a good
glue gun.

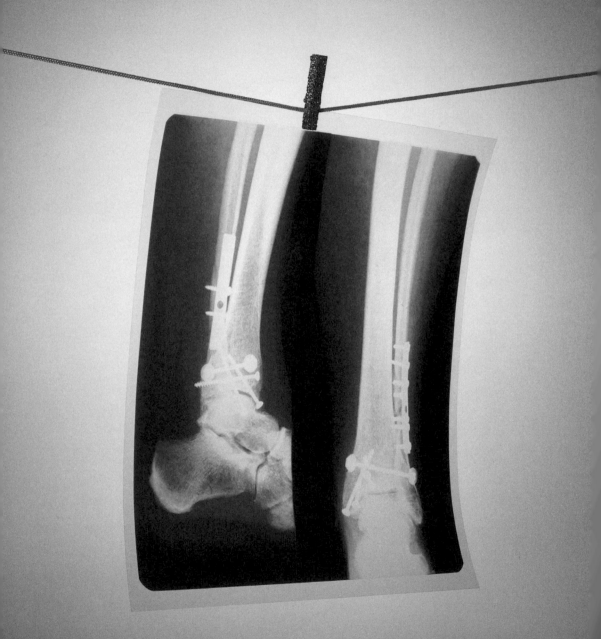

KIDS' CORNER:
What part of the
body do you think
this X-ray shows?

Design
EMMA
SCOTT-CHILD

HOW TO . . .

1.

2.
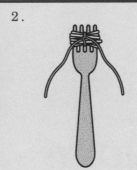

3.
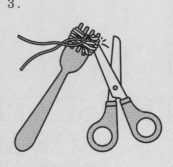

CUSTOMIZE A CRUTCH USING WOOL AND STICKY TAPE.

4.
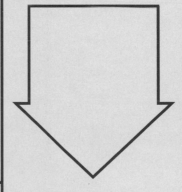

EQUIPMENT:
Different types of tape
(gaffer, masking, electrical,
washi)
Scissors
Dental floss
Wool
A fork
–
–
–
–
–

1. Make a pompom to hang from
the handle: Start by wrapping
a length of wool around a fork
approximately 20 times.

2. Tie the wool together
tightly around the middle using
dental floss—it's much stronger
than sewing thread.

3. Use nail scissors to snip
down either side of the wool to
release the pompom. Tuft it and
trim it with scissors to form a
nice ball shape.

4. Wrap a layer of tape around
the bottom of the crutch. You
can continue up the crutch
using different types of tape
for each layer, or you can
cover it all in masking tape
and draw directly onto it.

THE SHAPE
OF MEMORY:

Your child might inherit your looks.
They might also inherit the
way you look at yourself.

LIKE ANY EXPECTING parent, Hannah considered the variety of traits she'd hoped to pass down to her child: compassion; honesty; a tendency to laugh at even the lamest of dad jokes. One thing she knew she didn't want to pass on was her relationship with food. Hannah, 33, has struggled with disordered eating since she was a child. Growing up, her parents put great emphasis on healthy and organic foods, and would often make judgmental comments about other people's bodies or eating habits. Her mother would constantly diet and do aerobics; her father would tell her he was "being bad" or "didn't need this" if he ate dessert. Hannah was not allowed to eat fast food, soda or sugary cereals, so when visiting friends' houses, she would raid their junk food cabinets and binge.

"This eventually bloomed into full-blown anorexia in my 20s, after some traumatic life events," she says. "I ended up seeking help with an outpatient treatment team. Now, six years after treatment, I consider myself fully recovered."

But the fear of perpetuating the cycle of disordered eating remains. Hannah, who

asked that her last name be omitted, became a mom for the first time in 2020. And while pregnancy didn't spark any negative thoughts in relation to her own body, she fears she will inadvertently pass on the ideologies

she grew up with to her now six-month-old.

"Joking about food, diets and weight is so ingrained in the way that people socialize, especially women," she says. "I have found myself chuckling along to jokes in front of the baby that I later realized I would be horrified for him to hear. Now that I'm responsible for helping to shape the way someone sees the world, food and their body, I need to do the very best job possible of modeling healthy ideas."

When it comes to parenting, discussions surrounding body image, healthy eating habits and self-love center around the children. Caregivers are inundated with advice in this regard, but rarely are they encouraged to reckon with themselves and, in particular, their own childhood. Joseph Sacks, a psychotherapist specializing in child therapy and practicing in New York City, says it can be incredibly difficult for people to untether themselves from the "lessons" they learned growing up. In order to parent your own children in a thoughtful way, you have to "shatter the illusion that your [own] parents were perfect"—something Sacks says people don't often want to do. "In order to overcome the mistakes of your parents, you have to admit that your parents screwed up," he explains.

Liz Kleinrock
recommends Aubrey
Gordon's book
*What We Don't Talk
About When We
Talk About Fat* as
essential reading
on this topic.

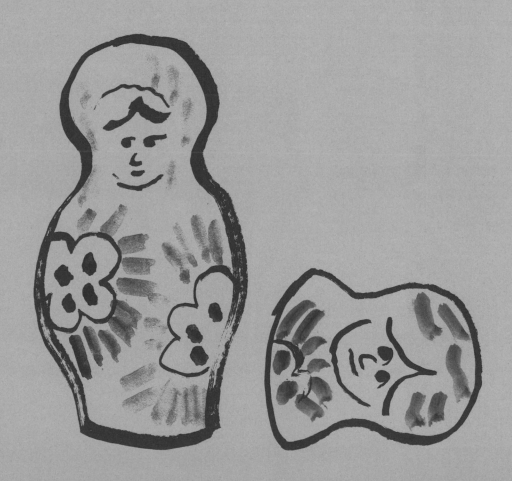

People tend to idealize their childhoods—and those who go on to have children often seek to recreate the moments they themselves would love to go back to. But it's not just the past that people crave: they often crave a version of the past that didn't exist. As people grow older, they don't hold on to a true recreation of the past, but rather a variety of memories melted together—a highlights reel rather than an accurate documentary.

Some parents or caregivers may want, even demand, that their child play a sport, recalling their athletic glory days while forgetting the pressure put on them by their own parents. Some may push specific dietary restrictions on their children, citing the rules they had to abide by as a child and crediting them for the health they enjoy today, forgetting how those same rules made them feel about their innate desires for certain foods or how their body looked at various stages throughout adolescence. For others, it's the more painful memories of the past that guide their parenting. In an attempt to shield their children from the very situations they had to overcome, caregivers may overcompen-

sate. "Sometimes the parent recognizes what their parents did was wrong, but makes a mistake with their child trying to compensate for something," Sacks says. "Let's say if one parent was overweight as a kid and ate too much junk food and had a lot of trouble, they'll say, 'I know what the problem is: my parents let me have too much junk food, too much junk food is the problem. So they don't let them have any junk food, so the kid is desperate and obsessed with junk food for the rest of their life."

Whichever way the pendulum swings, the prescription is broadly the same: try to reflect honestly and compassionately on what you're bringing to the table from your own childhood, so you can understand where certain impulses come from. For Travis Harper, 34, it is the painful memories of his childhood that have, at times, informed his parenting. Upon entering the third grade he quickly became "the pudgy kid." His peers would tease him and poke his stomach. When Travis told his parents, who were also overweight, about his treatment at school, they said his siblings had endured the same taunts and that, with time, it would pass. Now, Travis is a father to a nine-year-old son, and can't help but reconsider his own experience as his child enters pre-teenhood. His son was born with Pectus excavatum, a condition in which a person's breastbone is sunken into their chest. Travis knows the condition alone could lead to body image issues for his son, even without any added ideas around weight, dieting and food. "I don't want my son to have to struggle with looking at himself in the mirror like I did," he says, "or to think that he's less of a person because of the way he looks."

But Travis knows in order to do that he must reconcile with his past and his feelings about his own body. When he noticed that his son had put on some weight in addition to growing taller, he couldn't help but comment on his eating habits. "I once actually had the audacity to tell him that he needs to not be grazing as much because he doesn't want to end up fat like me. I realized immediately what I had said was wrong. I felt like garbage. I still do. Parenting is always a struggle, and it's hard enough raising kids not to have complexes from external sources, let alone giving them one yourself."

Countless studies have shown that children learn by example—they mimic what those closest to them do and say, learning from both their successes and their missteps. So

> "I've found myself chuckling along to jokes that I would be horrified for the baby to hear."

in wanting what's best for our children—a healthy relationship with food; a positive body image; self-love—we must want it for ourselves, too. Yet rarely are caregivers told to put themselves and their wellbeing first. Instead, the focus is on how they can do best for their child, not themselves. The parenting part of the person is cut off from their personhood, then prioritized above all. Finding the space to practice self-acceptance when society expects martyrdom is not only difficult—it's radical. And a pervasive and insidious diet culture, along with an obsession with athletic prowess and sexualized bodies, can make that radical act intensely exhausting.

For Hannah, she can honestly say that pregnancy and early parenthood have both given her a newfound love for herself and how she looks. "I am more in love with and grateful for my body than ever before," she says. "It got me through a difficult and high-risk pregnancy in a global pandemic, and grew the most beautiful and amazing little human being."

Still, she knows she has to remain alert. From journaling to consistent therapy to "talking with my husband and my family about what I will absolutely not accept being said to and around our child as he grows up," Hannah remains both vigilant and hopeful.

As for Travis, he says there's still work to be

done. He still holds unhealthy and unkind feelings about himself, and says it's a "constant struggle" to push those feelings aside or rectify them entirely. "But my child, they're the best thing to have ever come out of me, and I want them to be the very best version of themselves," he says. "I try to remind myself to see the world through his eyes, to see how my behavior may be affecting him." **k**

It's good to think consciously about what your child learns from you, but don't berate yourself for having complex life experiences of your own to work through. No one transforms into the perfect role model simply by virtue of having a child.

One of the most important proactive skill sets that caregivers can impart to their children is the ability to express and respect boundaries. While "consent" is often thought of as something tied to sexual or romantic relationships, it actually means to give permission. For children, understanding consent can include learning to reject demands for unwanted physical contact such as tickling or hugging, identifying adults to confide in if someone makes you feel uneasy or if you know someone who is being harmed, and recognizing the nuances of body language and tone when someone says "yes" but really means "no."

When we introduce language and tools around consent to young people, we are teaching them a powerful and important message: Your body is your own, and you get to decide what makes you feel comfortable or uncomfortable.

Question:

CAN YOU THINK OF SITUATIONS WHEN YOU NEED CONSENT FROM ANOTHER PERSON?

If you want to touch
....
someone's hair.
....

....

....

....

....

....

....

....

....

YES! NO. MAYBE...
Let's learn the language around consent.

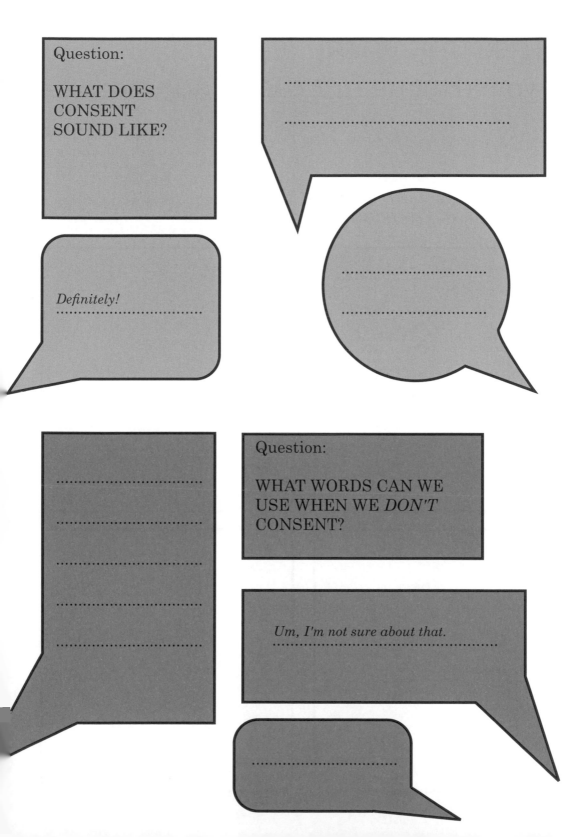

Question:

WHAT DOES CONSENT SOUND LIKE?

....
....

Definitely!
....

....
....

....
....
....
....
....

Question:

WHAT WORDS CAN WE USE WHEN WE *DON'T* CONSENT?

Um, I'm not sure about that.
....

....

PICTURE THIS!
Two cartoons in need of an ending.

Alex wants to give Jamie a hug, but Jamie isn't sure they want a hug right now. DRAW THEIR CONVERSATION.

Maya wants to dance with Spencer, but Spencer isn't sure they want to dance right now. Maya is annoyed because Spencer wanted to dance with them yesterday. DRAW THEIR CONVERSATION.

Educator Liz Kleinrock is part of our editorial board and the author of *Start Here, Start Now: A Guide to Anti-Bias and Anti-Racist Work in Your School Community*. Drawing comics about consent is an exercise she's done with her third grade students (eight- and nine-year-olds). As well as being a good way of testing their understanding of the concepts, it's a fun opportunity to practice writing dialogue.

Foo Foo

What's in a name? Confidence, pride and safety, says Anna Kosztovics, who got

Hoo Ha

Flower
Twinkle

Cookie
Thingy.

Sweden to agree on—and use—a common word for girls' genitals.

In 2006, the official dictionary of the Swedish language introduced a new word for girls' genitals. The term, *snippa,* is now used everywhere in Sweden as the female equivalent of *snopp,* or "willy," giving children and adults a neutral, connotation-free word to describe female anatomy. It's the legacy of Malmö-based social worker Anna Kosztovics, who started promoting the name in 50 local nurseries in 2000 in collaboration with the Swedish Association for Sexuality Education (RFSU). "It spread so quickly," she says. "Sweden is not that big a country, so maybe it wasn't that difficult." Still, the rapid uptake of this new bit of vocabulary—a process that can take decades—says a lot about Kosztovics' achievement in filling a long-standing language gap.

Kosztovics went on to write an illustrated book, *Snippor & Snoppa,* that teaches children about their bodies and sexuality, and introduces them to the many forms that gender identity can take, while the Swedish national broadcaster, SVP, made a song about the topic. With almost 10 million views on YouTube, the song—and Kosztovic's message—has taken Sweden by storm. "You know a snippa is really kind of cool. All the girls think it's excellent. Even graceful ladies think it's elegant," the lyrics go. Twenty years after she began her campaign, Kosztovics is still hoping that other countries will follow Sweden's example and confine "front bottoms" "minnies" and "fru-frus" to the dustbin of euphemism history.

AW: What word did you use for girls' genitals when you
AK: were little?

My dad said *misse,* which is a word for cat. He was Hungarian, so I think he just translated it from his native language. Nobody else used this term and I was embarrassed about it. My mum just never mentioned that part of the body. When I got older she once used "down there," but that was it.

AW: Was there the same taboo in your friends' families?
AK: Yes, there were so many words around, so the topic was often avoided entirely. Some of my friends' families used the term *kissen,* which comes from the verb "to pee." Others used *framstjärt,* meaning "front bottom," or *frammen,* "the front." Of course, there were also many dirty terms, but there wasn't one word that had no connotations. The options were either too clinical or too sexual.

AW: What was it like for boys?

"If you can't mention something
to others, you automatically think it's
something to be ashamed of."

The euphemism "vajayjay" was introduced into the popular lexicon via *Grey's Anatomy* because US censors insisted actors couldn't repeatedly say "vagina" during an episode about child birth.

AK: It was different. There was one word for "willy" that everyone used: snopp.

AW: Is that how the idea for snippa came about?

AK: Exactly. I was pregnant and was thinking, *If I'm going to have a girl, I need to know what to call her genitals, otherwise I couldn't live with myself.* I asked everyone around me what word they were using. One friend from the north of Sweden told me she was using snippa. She had heard it from her mum, who was working in a school there. I liked the name and so I started practicing saying it in front of the mirror.

AW: And did you have a girl?

AK: No, I had a boy! It's true that at first I thought, "I don't need this word then." But when my son was one and a half or two years old, he asked me, "Mama, where's your snopp?" Because I had thought about it and practiced it before, I didn't just say that I don't have a snopp. I said: "I have a snippa." It's not that I'm lacking something—that's how he would have understood it otherwise. It hit me then that it's just as important for boys to have a term for female genitalia as it is for girls.

AW: Why is that?

AK: If only girls know and use the name snippa, then there's still a taboo around it. It's important that we all have a word, even the adult community. Because if you can't mention something to others, you automatically think it's something to be ashamed of. My intention was to get rid of this shame surrounding female genitalia.

AW: Do you find that boys have the same feeling of shame about their willies?

AK: No, anybody who has a boy has probably experienced the pride that they feel about their snopp. My son, for example, he's proud of his penis, but he's also really proud when he scores a goal in football. All children need to be able to feel this: that they can be proud of many things, including their genitals.

AW: Would it have been possible to give girls the same sense of pride by using an anatomically correct term, such as vulva?

AK: Medical terms such as vulva or vagina are more commonly used in English than in Swedish, so that was less of an option in my case. I do believe though that if they are said in a friendly, positive way, they work, because we start associating them with something beautiful.

"It's just as important for boys to have a term for female genitalia as it is for girls. If only girls know and use the name *snippa* there's still a taboo around it."

AW: Why is it that in most languages we have so many words for genitalia and only a few words for arm, for example?

AK: There's more to your vulva than your arm. It's a taboo area. On the female body, there's the vulva, the vagina, and so on, and many people simply don't know one from the other. I don't think that it's just for reasons of shame though; there are so many euphemisms because we know that it's a special place.

AW: What are some of the strangest euphemisms that you've come across?

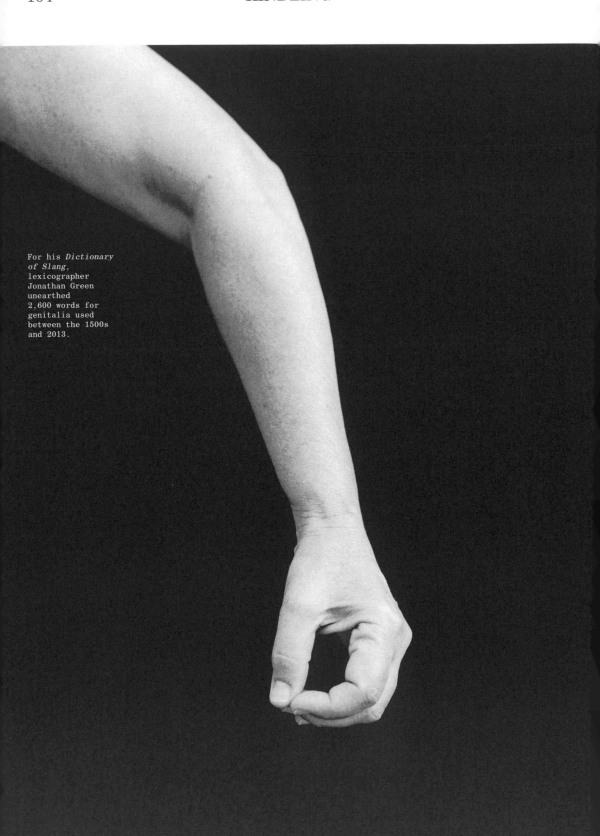

For his *Dictionary
of Slang*,
lexicographer
Jonathan Green
unearthed
2,600 words for
genitalia used
between the 1500s
and 2013.

His research
reinforces the
fact that words
matter: Throughout
the centuries, the
penis was most
commonly described
as a weapon and
the vagina as a
passive void.

AK: "Letterbox" and "summerhouse."

AW: How does your work intersect with trans identities in children?

AK: When interviewing nursery school teachers I found that 20% had seen children that identified as a different gender than the body they were born into. There are boys, for example, who will only play when they are wearing girls' clothes, or girls with short hair claiming to be boys. It's very important that adults allow children to express this.

AW: You have also done some wider research into child sexuality. Can you tell us a bit more about this strand of your work?

AK: The message is that we shouldn't stop or ignore children's sexual behavior. Someone working in a nursery

once told me that during nap time there was always at least one child touching their snopp or snippa. I didn't know about this, but I thought that people needed to know and understand that we are all sexual beings. It's natural. Funnily, snippa was just one element within my research, but it's the one that struck immediately. It's easier to say snippa than to talk about child sexuality.

It's natural for children to explore, but also important that they understand boundaries. The exercises on page 94 might be a useful resource.

AW: What's the strangest question a child has asked you?

AK: My son came home from nursery once asking me: "My friend calls her snippa *kissen* [from the Swedish kissa, 'to pee']. Does that mean that her bum is called 'poo'?"

AW: How should adults respond to these types of questions?

AK: Be open. If you start talking to children from an early age, they don't know society expects them to feel ashamed about certain body parts and sexuality. **k**

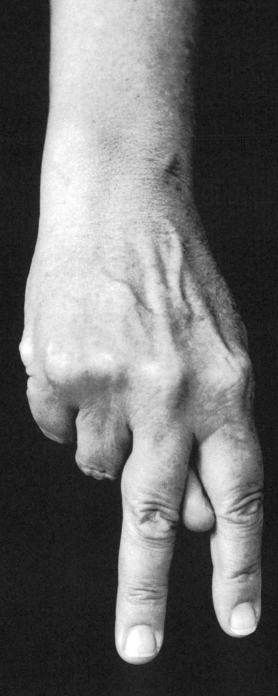

In English-speaking countries, there is a push to avoid cutesy euphemisms entirely and use anatomically correct terms for penis, testicles, vagina and vulva. The distinction between these latter two terms isn't always clearly understood, but important in this context: The vulva encompasses all external female genitalia, while the vagina is the canal leading to the cervix.

FUN STUFF

Activities by EMMA SCOTT-CHILD
& illustrations by ALBERT TERCERO

109 – 120

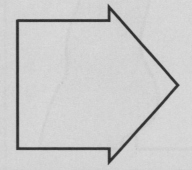

FIVE FUN GAMES TO OCCUPY THE NEXT FIVE MINUTES.

OPEN HERE IN CASE OF EMERGENCY

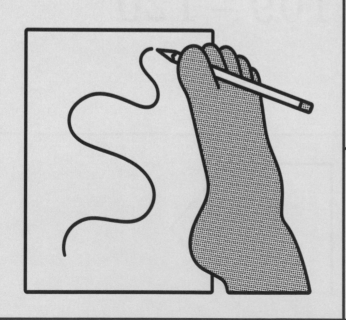

1. ALPHABET I SPY
See if you can spot things around you that start with each letter of the alphabet, beginning with A and working your way through to Z: An aerial, a brick, a crow, etc.

2. WHEN I'M IN CHARGE…
What would you do if you were the boss of the whole world? Would you make ice cream free for everyone? Would you build a tower to the moon? Would you make big corporations clean up the oceans? These plans are your policies. Get other people to come up with their own policies, and you can then vote for your favorite boss.

3. MEASURE YOUR BODY PARTS
Did you know that your body has lots of proportions that match up? Although every body will be a bit different, here are some things that might be true for you:

- Your arm span is equal to your height.

- Your foot is the same length as your forearm (from elbow crease to wrist crease).

- Your thumb is the length of your nose.

4. CLEVER FEET
Have you ever tried to draw with your feet? Have a go. Take your shoes and socks off and put a pencil between your big toe and the next one. Place a piece of paper on the floor and see if you can draw. It's tricky!

5. HAPPY HALF BIRTHDAY
You know when your birthday is, but what about your half birthday? A half birthday is exactly six months between your last birthday and your next one. Can you figure out which day it is?

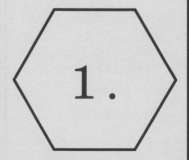

1.

USE YOUR BODY AS A CANVAS FOR SENSORY ART.

In 1971, the artist Dennis Oppenheim made a series of artworks with his son Erik. Erik drew on Dennis's back, and then Dennis simultaneously drew what he could feel on the wall. This is a really fun drawing activity that you can do with another person. See if you can communicate a picture to each other, using the sense of touch to create art together!

STROKE OF GENIUS

2.1

2.2

INSTRUCTIONS
—

2.1 Tape a piece of paper to one person's back, and another piece to the wall. It's best if you're wearing something light like a T-shirt. A sweater will be too thick.

2.2 Draw on the paper on the person's back: something simple like a line that they have to follow, or big bold shapes. The person who is having their back drawn on has to copy the drawing onto the paper on the wall using their sense of touch to guide them. See if the two drawings look the same. If you don't mind getting messy, you can use face paint sticks to draw directly onto the other person's back.

2.

DISCOVER ENDLESS PASTA-BILITIES FOR MODEL BUILDING.

Did you know you can build towers from things you find in your kitchen? Use this recipe to build a structure with homemade dough and either toothpicks or dried spaghetti.

LITTLE ARCHITECTS

3.1

3.2

3.3

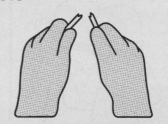

TO MAKE THE DOUGH, YOU'LL NEED:
-
  2 cups flour
  1 cup salt
  1 cup water
-
-

3.1 Mix the flour, salt and water in a bowl until you have a thick dough.

3.2 Roll small pieces of dough between your palms to make tiny little balls, each around the size of a pea. (It might look tasty, but don't eat the dough. It has a lot of salt in it because salt is a great preservative that helps the dough to dry.)

3.3 If you're using spaghetti, snap it into sticks that are about two and a half inches long. It helps if all the pieces are the same length.

3.4 Create shapes by joining the balls with the sticks. Start by making some squares and triangles, then branch out into 3D shapes.

3.

3.4

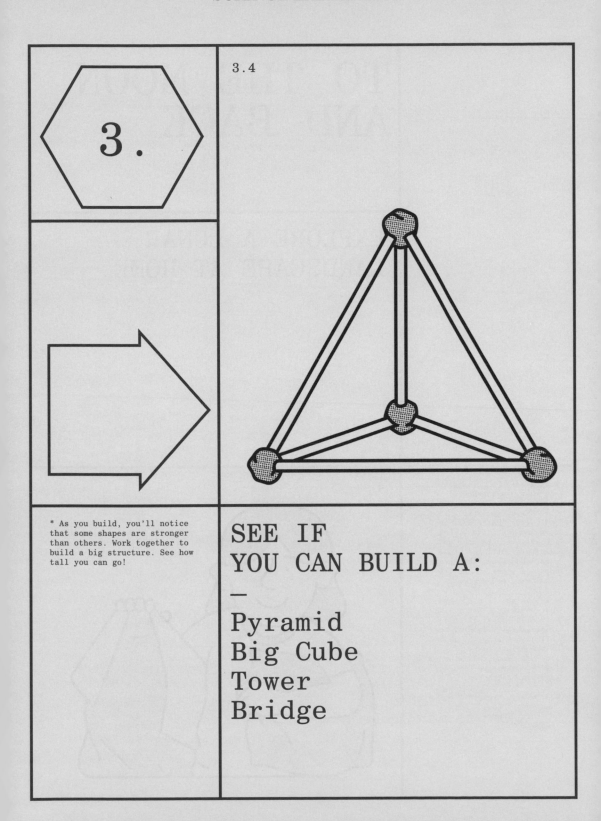

* As you build, you'll notice that some shapes are stronger than others. Work together to build a big structure. See how tall you can go!

SEE IF
YOU CAN BUILD A:
—
Pyramid
Big Cube
Tower
Bridge

TO THE MOON AND BACK

EXPLORE A LUNAR LANDSCAPE AT HOME.

Take a trip to outer space and see what you can find.

4.1 First, get some sheets and duvets. White ones feel more moonish. Spread them out all over the floor and furniture until the whole room is covered, then place cushions under the sheets to make bumps and craters.

4.2 Now you'll need some space helmets. Take a bike helmet and cover it in aluminum foil, folding the foil around into the inside of the helmet to keep it attached. You could also add a few antennae pipe cleaners, or some big headphones.

4.3 Sit on a chair and countdown from 10 until blastoff! Your rocket has flown into space.

4.1

THINGS TO DO ON THE MOON:

Practice walking like there's not so much gravity.

Have a picnic! The moon looks a bit like it's made of holey cheese, so that could be a good thing to eat.

Watch out for aliens disguising themselves as pets or babies. Take notes on these strange creatures to report back home.

Can you build a space station on the moon? You'll need a base camp for all of your scientific experiments.

Make a flag to mark your territory. What is the name of your space agency?

Some of your soft toys might like to visit you on the moon. You could make helmets for them using small boxes and foil.

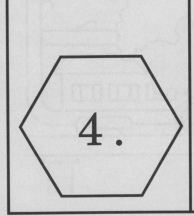

4.2

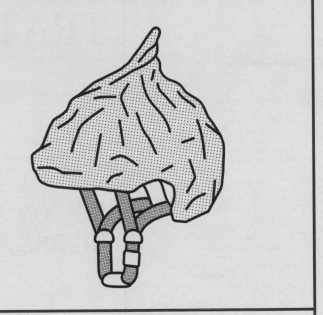

4.3

Explorers have used maps for thousands of years and we still use them today to help us make sense of the world around us. There are all sorts of different maps, not just those showing roads. Indigenous people in some parts of Australia, such as the Warlpiri, traditionally drew detailed patterns in the sand to clearly mark out their land and territories. For centuries, sailors created diagrams of the night sky to navigate from one side of the world to the other using the stars. Some maps use colors to show us the temperature in different parts of the world and some use lines to represent varying heights; this is called a topographic map.

Next time you're on a boring train, pretend you're an explorer and make a map of your trip. As you travel, make notes of what you see along the way and draw them on your map. Maybe you could invent new names for the places you see. For instance, if you stop at a station where you see someone wearing a hat, you could name that place "Hatville." Have fun and make it as weird as you like.

As you go along your journey, draw the things you see. You might see a pink house, a funny dog or a really cool tree. If you go through an area with lots of trees, you could color an area of your map green, or if you see lots of little square houses you could fill that part of the map with little squares. On your way back, have a look at your map and trace your journey back. Can you predict what's coming up next by looking at the map?

TRAIN TIME

DRAW A MEMORY MAP ON YOUR NEXT JOURNEY.

5.

A GOOD IDEA FOR BAD WEATHER.

RAIN DRUMS

6.

There are lots of cozy things to do inside on a rainy day, but what if we went outside and played in the rain? The rain can awaken our senses. We can feel it on our skin, and even taste it! Stick your tongue out and catch some raindrops. Depending on where you live, rainy weather might even have its own particular smell because it makes the ground and plants release different scents.

For this activity, we're going to use the rain to make some music.

Take some pots and pans outside and place them upside down like little drums. The raindrops will make sounds as they hit the pans. See how it gets louder as the raindrops get heavier. You could add some plastic containers to see if the sound is any different.

If you want to be really rock and roll, use some wooden spoons as drumsticks and join in with a freeform percussion performance.
—

DESIGN

A – Z

AREAWARE
areaware.com

ARKET
arket.com

BURBERRY
burberry.com

ENTIREWORLD
theentireworld.com

FINNISH DESIGN SHOP
finnishdesignshop.com

HAY
hay.com

JOHN LEWIS
johnlewis.com

K-WAY
k-way.com

MARKS & SPENCER
marksandspencer.com

NIKE
nike.com

OFF-WHITE
off---white.com

RALPH LAUREN
ralphlauren.com

STUDIO ROOF
studioroof.com

TEKLA
teklafabrics.com

UNIQLO
uniqlo.com

WITHINGS
withings.com

YOTO
us.yotoplayer.com

PP. 18–19
OFFLINE LEARNING
Years Don't Wait for Them, Human
Rights Watch, May 2021

2:1
*COVID-19 and learning loss—
disparities grow and students
need help*, McKinsey Institute,
December 2020

WI-FI ON WHEELS
*These buses bring school to
students*, The New York Times,
December 2020

$789.49
Annual Survey, National Retail
Federation, December 2020

PP. 34–44
Models: Blue and Jacob at KIDS
LONDON

— **Ducks in a Row**
The *Kindling* birds learn all about the bees.

Words & Art
SARAH HINGLEY